Joan Colby
SELECTED POEMS

FUTURECYCLE PRESS

Hayesville, North Carolina

Published by FutureCycle Press
Hayesville, North Carolina, USA

ISBN 978-1-938853-29-6

For Alan

Contents

From
BLUE WOMAN DANCING IN THE NERVE

From
THE BOUNDARY WATERS

From
HOW THE SKY BEGINS TO FALL

From
DEAD HORSES

Foreword

Joan Colby first published in *Spoon River Quarterly* the winter of 1979, my second number as editor of that journal. In the fall '79 *SRQ*, I had cleaned out all the weak poems accepted by the previous editor; the hidden agenda for winter was to make it a showcase issue and distribute it free to Midwest libraries and poets as an example of what *SRQ* could really do. Over the next few years, *SRQ* published a dozen more of Colby's poems: I especially liked her complex metaphors and her candid sexuality, which was a throw-back to the high sixties, quite at odds with the neo-Victorian academic feminism of my own academic world. (Perhaps Colby understands sexuality because she hangs around horses and not the Sociology or Literature Department.) Even when borrowing from Marc Chagall or Greek mythology, Colby describes life as I live it, writing of the "*nature* of Greek myths." The line "all true emeralds are illicit" had a particular appeal to me in my forties...like the image of mates drowning in each other's arms. (Later, in February of 1987, after a very successful and well-attended reading at my college, Southwest Minnesota State University, Colby elaborated on her poetry with some hard but life-saving advice which, notes remind me, "cleaned out whole truckloads of shit from my head.")

Spoon River Poetry Press published two books of Joan Colby's poetry. The first, *How the Sky Begins to Fall* (1982), was part of another hidden agenda: double a book with an issue of *Spoon River Quarterly*, on the one hand reducing the problem of finding sixty-four pages of good poetry four times a year, and on the other, giving the author wider audience. The book-as-quarterly would also show subscribers what good poetry is all about: in this case a close look at the all-too-familiar dance between men and women, with all its subtle desires, fears, and complex ambiguities. In 1986, as I passed editorship of *SRQ* to Lucia Getsi, Spoon River Poetry Press published another Joan Colby book, *The Lonely Hearts Killers*.

Now, in 2013, Joan Colby offers us her *Selected Poems*. Thirty-five years is a long time in anyone's career — long enough to see how things turned out. Long enough to allow us to draw some conclusions. Long enough to trace the arc of a career, to notice foreshadowings of late work in early poems and echoes of early work in later poems. As Eliot once observed,

"In my beginning is my end," and "In my end is my beginning."

For this reason, it's sometimes best to begin a *Selected Poems* collection at the book's end. Colby's poem "The Lunar Year" is as good a starting point as any: the poem tracks life through "Hunger Moon," when love and potatoes fail, through "Strawberry Moon," when the pasture fills with sweet rubies, to "Harvest Moon," with her cornucopia of fulfillment, to "Wolf Moon," when the predators return. Along the way, Colby touches on themes that have occupied her throughout this book: the ruthlessness of love, the connectedness of all creatures (human and otherwise), the wisdom of youth and the wisdom of maturity, "the lust that glues two lovers," and the iron paradigm of dreams and failed dreams. Living out on the prairie as I do, and suspicious as I am of cities, and envisioning, like Bob Dylan, some impending Armageddon, I especially like Colby's conclusion:

> They have come back, those predators
> Of the prairie, the steppe, the open range.
> Protected as a parliament
> Of oligarchs. Their guard hairs rising
> As they sight you, out there
> In your unarmed villages.

Not without reason is Colby's next poem titled "Roadkill."

Disaster, Colby has warned us throughout her career, is the nature of life. Grandfather was transformed from an ordinary forebear into a legend because he was shot five times and killed somewhere on the Utah frontier. Father studied theories of creation and dissolution in the stars. Colby—or her persona in these poems—enters warily into the lists of love...as does her partner. Love does not always prevail, and sweetness is not to be trusted. The roof leaks, and in dreams a twister opens the house like a coffin lid. "We talk divorce." Out in the world, wells run dry, and then rivers. Barns catch fire. Cattle die, and horses. And, of course, childhood dreams.

Then there are the truly evil disasters lurking out there: the lonely hearts killers and the just plain killers. The brewers of atrocities, from five-year-old suicides to crocodile ladies to the holy martyrs—"Catherine and her wheel, Joan and the pyre." The random accidents of a trucker shot from an adjacent stall as he urinates, the man killed trying to rescue ducklings on the tollway. "None of these people were wicked," Colby notes in "The Disaster Plan." John Irving's "undertoad" (*The World According to Garp*) and the grotesque have been prominent features of Colby's poetry since early on (see especially "Water Babies"), presumably because they are prominent features of nature and human nature. Rain and darkness have been dominant images in Colby's poetry since her earliest work. The wilderness will never be tamed. Plundering and looting owls, coons, lizards, crows overlook the landscape always. Roadkill is everywhere. Clio, the goddess of history, creates her textbook from one human disaster after another and drowns men in shallows of phosphorescent water. Today's feel-good society needs to grasp this fact.

But the news is not all bad. Paradoxically, in these poems dark rain is also where love begins...or sex, out of which love grows. Perhaps this is the case because Colby grounds her analysis in nature and in mythology based on nature. Certainly the dark complexities of male-female relationships account for the ambiguity which is so prominent in this book, which was so compelling in *How the Sky Begins to Fall*. What we learn growing up, Colby tells us, is not clarity but uncertainty: "I've lost that brevity,/ that arrogance/ of what is what," she admits in "Processes," written for her first book. "Open your arms to winter and everything holy or bleak," she suggests at the close of a later poem commemorating the loss of childhood dreams. Returning from a read through *Selected Poems* to the book's beginning, we note that the first poem here — "Morning in Late October" — is a seesaw back and forth between pluses (golden notes, sumac thickets) and minuses (urine-soaked straw, the wind's polished knife) in the day and the human situation. There's Rose Red and there's Snow White, Nigh Ox and Off Ox, the dualities I mentioned earlier in "The Lunar Year."

While Colby's themes and closeness to nature have remained more or less consistent, her poetic technique has altered somewhat over the course of three decades. She has always avoided dialogue in the Dave Etter tradition, but her recent work moves from dense imagistic collages to a more narrative style, whether she's describing a threshing bee and steam show or a team of oxen at Garfield Farm. A sense of communal and family history — not entirely absent from early poems — is more prominent in later poems, as is a movement away from the guardian wings of the four evangelists, an eclectic assortment of religions. It also seems to me that the sense of loss and futility increases, as it does in late Bob Dylan and late all of us. We come to understand the vanity of human wishes. Still Colby tells us that we should never give up, that there is hope after despair, life after death, life even in — well, not in death, but in fear and anxiety.

—David Pichaske

David Pichaske, editor-publisher of Spoon River Poetry Press, teaches English at a Minnesota state university. He has received four years of Fulbright fellowships to Poland, Latvia, and Mongolia. He has published two dozen textbook-anthologies, histories, collections of his own poetry, and books of cultural and literary criticism, including *Beowulf to Beatles* (1971), *A Generation in Motion* (1979), *Late Harvest: Rural American Writing* (1991), *Poland in Transition* (1994), *The Father Poems* (2005), *Rooted: Seven Midwest Writers of Place* (2006), *Song of the North County: A Midwest Framework to the Songs of Bob Dylan* (2010), and most recently *Ghosts of Abandoned Capacity* (2012). He lives in a century-old farm house on the banks of the Minnesota River.

Joan Colby
SELECTED POEMS

From

BLUE WOMAN DANCING IN THE NERVE

Alembic Press, 1979

Morning In Late October

The sky is the navy blue
of a schoolgirl's uniform.
Norway maples bugle
golden notes
as wind pushes the stable door
like the calloused hand
of my grandfather. In the loose
box the appaloosa thuds,
wanting grain, the grey colt lips
my hands. My son, small for his 8 years,
bridles the tall chestnut mare.
The smell of urine-soaked straw and manure
infests the aisle where a dim light seeps
through a streaked overhead pane.
At my feet, the dog licks herself.

A cold blast greets us
when we emerge. The fields
are the color of ripe wheat,
the low hills purple. My son,
forked on his mare, leads
the way. I follow, ducking
the wind's polished knife,
the bay gelding shuddering
between my thighs.

The road winds
into a sumac thicket
bright as a hemorrhage.
The sky bruises, the maples howl
like a pack of yellow hounds
pursuing the new moon
still hanging in the slate-blue east
like a parenthesis.

Water Babies

My father is reading the story.
Paper birches shiver on the bank.
The dock runs out
plank by plank
to where the water darkens.

The sun capsizes in the lake,
its long glittering wake
pointing like a finger to the shore
where our cottage moors
in a vat of spruce,
a dark and liquid place
beset by sighs.

The harsh roar
of my father's voice
gutters in the quaver
of kerosene lamps.

This story is full of darkness.

I think of the sunfish
swallowing my hook,
its anguished silver flop
desequinning under my knife.

The antique light
flickers in its cage
like a wild bird.

The rafters
hold a wealth of darkness
in their roughened arms
where spiders suspend
and sharp things rustle.
A darkness
pokes into the snout of every flower,
slipping about the bole of every tree

while the lake grows immense,
a vast black bowl

the night keeps pouring into,
brimming with stars.

I dread
going up to bed alone—
the vigilance of rafters,
the square ogre eyes
of the windows,
the doorknob with its ghastly brass nose.

So I beg for one more chapter
of this story I'm not listening to,
that is over my head,
that will slide
from under my bed,
thick and cold
as a fish,
or a monstrous baby
with gill-slits and protuberant
lidless eyes
and bubbles coming from its lips
like words I can't pronounce,
terrors I can't voice.

The Helper

Riding along behind shafts of light,
he dozes while the driver
talks and talks,
the young wife sleeping
in a black contained silence
like the .38 erect along his thigh.

He dreams of the people in the fields
living in lean-tos and the Indians last winter
huddling around an oil drum's
smoky fire. How a woman double-crossed
by her own arms shuddered
when the wind picked up at sundown.

If he wakes he will see the trucker
steering through a muscular darkness,
the girl curled away,
her hands enclosing the deformity of her face.

He will think himself fortunate
to be hurtling through the dark land
without effort. Tomorrow in Albuquerque
he will help unload.

If he could know that tomorrow
the trucker will be shot from an adjacent stall
as he urinates,
that the young wife will vanish
like the people in the fields
or the Indians in winter,
what could he think about
unless it is the ornate brass
buckle cinching his Levis
or the Latigo boots he got
in El Paso last spring.

White Lilacs

The white lilac has a hundred ghostly fingers.
It points at the first stars.
It points at me
standing in a May twilight
with barbed wire hooking the darkness where
barbs of stars bloom astonishingly.

The cones of the white lilac
shake in a dark wind from the south.
Fragrance rattles
into air, odor of sweet
bones, night-mouths.

All night the lilacs will shudder here
at the edge of the meadow while
stars dazzle the sky's bush—
that black bush of menace.

A ghost
walks over my grave as my flesh rises.
The roots of the lilacs
strive through my skull, discovering the holes
I gaze out of. Existence
is terrible. The white lilacs
tremble as I tremble,
departing into themselves,
into their clusters of oneness,
refusing to be a symbol,
admitting nothing.

Clio Invents Her Textbook

The pages are parchment flayed
from the abdomens of dancing girls.
The spine is made of cartilage
extracted from the knees of senators
which is bound with the sinews
of charwomen and glued
with the bone-marrow jelly
of newborn children.

The covers are of tanned hide
stripped from circus strongmen,
and the gilt is from the teeth
of executives. The pages were cut
with the tongues of gossip columnists
and the woodcuts blocked
out of the dreams of virgins.

Now I begin
my story with a pen
that was the forefinger
of a teacher of anthropology
dipped in the blood
of convicted arsonists.

I form the first stroke
which is the shape of a dagger or a pillar,
which can be read as
a numeral or the self,
which meets the invisible
baseline of character and stops.

From here I go on
inscribing everything, everything,
without sequence, in a massive pastiche.

You will search these pages
all your life,
looking for your name.

Clio Psychotic

You undress for blind men and
whisper secrets into the padlocked ears of the deaf.
Clio, your body is the map
of a world that falls away
sharply at the horizon. Touch
The only landfall you honor.
Beyond the stars
your name dissolves like a meteor
encountering the logic of gravity.
Explosions bloom like magenta flowers along the circuits
of your flesh. A solo eye
peers into the cell of mattresses
where you begin to die into otherness.

O Tireless
Stenographer, imagine the pages
you have transcribed anonymously
until nightfall kindles dives and dramshops
to a neon bonfire
where you dance
deliriously in the eyes of lushes
intoxicated with your pretense
of style. Schizophrenic
stripper teasing the boozy masses.
You narrow toward daylight
effacing yourself.

Your résumé promises lessons
reflecting the future.
The credentials you list
are impressive and useless.
Mad Girl, your eel smile
flickers, a cave of Platonic deceits.
Imagine tomorrow—but backward
glancing's your system.
The trouble we borrow
can never be repaid. You laugh in your sleeve.
Psychopathic liar.
Loving us all for nothing.

Clio Takes You As Her Lover

See how she touches you. This is the way
you've dreamed of being seduced.
Slipping utterly
out of your will into your body.
Her fingers confuse
your sense of origins. All that you tried to know
seems absurd. Let her invent it for you
as she invents pleasure, the spiral nerve
that courses through your flesh,
night-blooming vine,
moon of seven madonnas.

Desire all of her faces. Alecto who never rests,
jealous Megaera, Tisiphone
who avenges...winged and snaky women.
Also Aglaea the splendid,
Euphrosyne, giver of joy. Thalia,
queen of pleasure. A Trinity
of graces.

You kiss her mouth. In the mirror
something flies toward you
like a flock of cranes.
You tremble. The Eumenides
are trying on your shadow.
She slides her lithe body
upon yours. You drown in shallows.
Phosphorescent water
glitters your eyes like tears.

It's conceivable she talks too much.
Your head whirls over breakfast.
Love defies analysis, you tell her.
She falls silent. Her long nails inscribe
a swastika on your chest. She pastes
a star between your eyes, says
she will burn her diary.

You're in love again. You ask
nothing from her but this:
that you lie all night in her arms.

She tosses her dice. Snake Eyes.
You win. You lose
yourself entirely.

Crazy Rain

Twilight.
The dull insanity of rain.

Your mother is telling ghost stories
to the wind. Her words are lost
like indulgences that caused the great split of faith.
You remember for the first time in years
the act of contrition you repeated like a charm
before sleeping. You were a child then
with nothing to be sorry for. The rain
taps the glass, its black fingers
burgling your dreams. It is the stranger
at the door asking directions.
You shoot the bolt. Trust was the first thing
you were missing. Then love saying its name
against the crack in the window.
But it sounded wrong. It sounded
like a scheme. Someone was trying to get in.
You nailed the boards
over those openings. Only the rain
swiveled through the fish-scale roof,
taking the way
of least resistance. Now it draws
a silhouette of loss on the ceiling
over your bed. Those four posts,
the evangelists. You slept in their
care under the guardian wings
of angels plucked
for your comforter.

You're no child any longer.
The child you were
cringes from this sentence and grows small
as a comma.
Each impersonation of the mirror
frightens you. The bone and ash
of your ancestors. The name you sign.
The ghost
in your head who suddenly remembers.

The rain is unfeeling. It pits the earth.
The earth is unfeeling too.
What are you doing here
expecting to be loved.

It rains, it rains
like crazy.

Processes

Ten years ago
I was writing poems
brief as bird tracks.

A wing
encapsulated an entire spring.

Three morning grace notes
scored all summer.

A single beak
bit off autumn like a worm.

A few hieroglyphs
on the snow
said everything there was
to know of winter.

I was younger then.
I was more certain.

All my short spare poems
knotted themselves into a final word
    like a crow shot from a tree.

But I've lost that brevity,
that arrogance
of what is what,
and my poems
flock like blackbirds
gleaning word after word,
line after line
from the waving field.

They are still famished,
cawing terribly in my mind.
I don't know what to give them.
I keep on writing
and writing.

Fugue With Two Crows

Two crows alight on a topmost branch,
unkempt as old trappers,
their black ragbags clutched
like stolen money.

Three months' hard freeze. Today:
a thaw. Further on, the river croons beneath
its lacy coverlet of ice like
a revived baby.

It shakes a rattle of bone.
Abandoned child
of cannibals.

Every roof looses its frozen tear.
So much pent-up feeling,
the snow has grown ancient and grey with it.

The crows
overlook the landscape.
Plunderers. Looters.
The windows of ice are cracking on every lake.
The small fish cruising
in gangs learn the sense of grab,
the rule of blood. How the willows
bend into jigsaw water
like native women whose sons wandered off,
lured by the river-goddess
in her sinuous and fitful bed.

A harsh cry
stabs through the trees'
stupor. The crows
flap off into the sleet
that begins its downfall of needles.
What heavy birds! Sad black hearts!
The hinges of their wings seem to groan
like the rheumatic branches. Even my eyes
ache with the freight
of their passing.

From

THE BOUNDARY WATERS

Damascus Road, 1982

The Boundary Waters

In front of the campfire
I'm reading a book on the nature of Greek myths,
but it's hard to concentrate.
I've come down the Granite River today
to Gunflint Lake
and I'm bone-tired, shoulders
aching from the bow-stroke.

The wind hectors the jackpines
as the split logs catch and burn.
My mind, rescued like Persephone,
melts in a mouth of blue flame.

Yet the underworld
ripens, a pomegranate
in my heart,
the wish to reduce
the world to words.

The fire smokes, then flares
as I toss on more birchbark.
The air chills
outside the flame's sway.

The wilderness
breathes at my back
like a vast black animal
that will never be tamed
by legend.

Looking straight up
the channel of tall birch,
I see the white inviolable
bonfire of one star.

Lullaby for Benjamin

You were born on Holy Thursday.
Easter, the nurses brought you
done up in rabbits ears
but I saw through that,
remembering how you gushed out
in a shroud of blood,
your sternum jutting like a handle,
your face screwed up as if the light
hurt you.

They laid you on my belly
as your feedbag, squeezed
out of my vagina, a slippery
red wombat.

I heard your screams
when they hauled you off to slice
away your foreskin. I struggled
but they held me. After all,
I'd authorized this thing before
I even knew your sex.

You sucked
like the devil at my breast,
red and thirsty
with a mouth made for rooting
and eyes that fastened on mine
to engage my heart, my pity.

A howler
no arms could comfort,
you stiffened and waved your fists
in a terrible protest.

Eight years later, you sit
at the table putting together
a jigsaw puzzle of the world
you fought against entering.

My youngest child—
too old to believe in the Easter Bunny,
too young to know that monsters
are not what will really hurt you.
I can't allay the fears
that notch your nightmares
like the toy gun you insist on sleeping with,
your fingers curled around the trigger
as your body rediscovers
its fetal position. I still
am heavy with you.

The Sugar Cure

All of your remedies, mother,
relied on sugar. A cube soaked with kerosene
to cure a sore throat. Mashed
into a paste with soap to draw a boil.
Spliced into poultice with onions
for pleurisy. You mixed whiskey
and sugar to ease colds a green winter breeds,
foretelling how such weather
feeds graveyards. You spread butter and sugar
on bread for an invalid's treat.

All that time, mother, your mouth screwed
into the tartness of unripe persimmons,
wrinkling with impoverished axioms:

> *Don't listen to sweet talk.*
> *Don't be a fool.*
> *Don't let your love blind you.*
> *Don't wear your heart on your sleeve.*

All those years, your grey eyes tarnishing
like the silver spoon extending sugar
to absolve the bitter necessary herbs.

When I was small, you gave me a twist of cloth
soaked in milk and sugar to suck my tears
dry as your heart—that immense cavity,
victim of the sweetness you couldn't trust,
an erosion that etched your proverbs
with black like funeral cards
bearing the names of the living.

Hoarfrost

The appaloosa grazes a glazed field.
A twist of branches
risks its signature.
The sky's a blank.

Desultorily, the horse
divines the pattern of its hunger.
A hawk
plummets from the crown of a burr-oak.
Something dies
without fanfare.

Sleet falls. A rain of blind needles.
A speechless wind. The gibbous rise
of headlands to the east
black with menace.

Pour your eyes
into this landscape. Now you'll move slowly
as the appaloosa working his way
across the silver pasture
mouthful by mouthful.

Penance

You can't be sorry
enough with words.
How can we tell you feel it
in the bone marrow, in the eye-socket,
simply because you say it?

Therefore you will
have to sit in the desert 40 years
dressed in camel dung,
sleeping on thorns,
eating nothing but snail slime
and guano.

When you return
prophesying, your hair wild
as a flock of startled birds,
your eyes red as an arroyo
carved by tears,
we'll take you in,
feed you,
let you lie down on silk
and examine your conscience.

Belles-Lettres

When your lover left you for another
woman you went out and bought
envelopes with a silver lining
and letter paper with a pattern of fluffy clouds
on mild blue. Then you sat down
to write a letter in invisible ink
with your new pen that resembles an index finger.

You pasted a stamp
with a picture of an endangered bird
on the corner of the envelope.
You dropped it in a box
that vandals had bashed and thrown
in an empty lot.

Then you walked away.
He is almost asleep now and your letter
is sailing through the slot of his eyes.

Salt

Carry salt in your hand when passing
from room to room in the dark.
The wife of your friend holds out her arms.
The salt of your tongue anoints her.

She looks back stiffening
at the destroyed city of fidelity,
sighing in your embrace.
Now you've betrayed everyone.

Bless yourself with Holy Water.
These elements
were consecrated separately,
then combined,
just as your bodies became one body
briefly in declining waves.

Once salt was money, friendship,
kept evil from the house.
To spill it signified a great misfortune.

You spill yourself in her
gasping as luck
twists its noose about you.
A hundred birds startle
from your pupils. To capture them,
you must salt their tail feathers.
You must offer salt to the angels
of your right hand.

This woman, now,
curls against you, brackish.
You want to flow
back to the seas of origin,
leaving the salt-flats
of her body, those white acres
burning beneath the moon.

Emeralds

All true emeralds are illicit.
Green stones
passed from hand to hand like beautiful women.
Secreted in the packs
of natives coming down from the highlands.
Whispered in cafes in Bogota,
a cold fire in palms
of couriers.

A man ascends
the moon-ladder of a woman's thighs.
They prize love beyond diamonds.
They penetrate customs.

When he abandons her,
her eyes grow mineral. Deep in earth
of her heart something winks,
green and rare as a phenomenal
tropical sunset.

Imagine the time
it took to squeeze perfection
from flesh and blood. The gem
they risked everything for
smuggled over the borders
of their bodies.
How rich they were.

The Sea-Changes

The calculus of this story
smashes through silent water
like a blue torpedo.

You are the sailor
swabbing the decks with blood,
eye on the sun for weather
and navigation. At night the stars
command your attention. The Southern Cross
falling from your sextant like the old religion
until Polaris rises immobile,
a true calling.
What will you become
when the sea casts you up
from its cold green amazements?
You practice all the knots
of your trade. Contemplate the ports
ravishing with dark women
who slam castanets over your body
or slide silver knives
from between their thighs.

A sailor's dreams
always steer landward
like suicidal whales
beset by parasites of the inner ear
who sing with the unmistakable voice
of the Lorelei. I write the chanty
of your life until its nose blunts with explosives
against your ribcage. You think
it is simply your heart racing
at the sight of a mermaid
or one of the fabulous serpents
who lurk at the edges of maps.

We are in the fatal horse latitudes now,
listening to the white hooves
crashing upon the hull,

thinking of the lifeboats
that will never bear us to safety,
the ballast shifting
irretrievably under our sleep.

Jettisoning all precious
cargo before we wake
like mates drowning
in the arms of each other.

Wilderness Camp

All day on Muskellunge Lake,
the cold wind dividing whitecaps
upon the bow of our canoe,
the sky terrifyingly blue,
pine and birch an audience
whose reaction we can't guess,
we sit anchored out and fish.

Paddling in the red
corpuscles of sunset,
our stringers trailing perch
through silver-varnished currents,
we home in to our campfire
with scaling knives and cornmeal,
crouch in a wigwam blaze,
eating with our fingers,
thinking we see those selves
whose civilization blinds us
charring in blue flame.

Embers of another
fire across the inlet,
a voice winging the water,
racing toward our deaths. My ancestors
went at 60, that's about
what I expect.

We see the bulk of his shadow
cross his dying flame
and know he's making the motions
of readying for night
the same
as us.

Silence moving in
off the lake
in a cold blast
as the banked fires smolder
beneath a bad-axe moon

and we sleep, or try to,
in nests of down
like fledglings
while the owl hunts
and the coon
rustles our leavings.

From

HOW THE SKY BEGINS TO FALL

Spoon River Poetry Press, 1982

Detecting Love

Inveigle me with dark rain.
I embrace the blacklist
headed with my name. I creep
through the Pentagon like a spy
speaking seven languages,
none of them my own.

Examine the bone of my hip,
its exquisite machinery.
Tell me any story
you care to invent.

It is the end of the month,
the rent is due, the landlord
suspects we have given refuge
to wild cats. Paper the windows
with paychecks. All of our money,
like all of our love, is overdue.

Pretend I am a gumshoe lurking
in the wet neon,
tailing you and your blonde
pick-up-sticks. Let's imagine
your tempo is like the rain,
dissembling but violent
wherever the rivers toss
in narrow beds.

If I were a grand piano
in a concert hall, I'd set my ivory teeth
into your flesh, making you scream with music
as if Beethoven leaped feet-first through glass.

If you were knocking
on storm doors seeking shelter from this rain,
I'd open up like the woman of your dreams:
voluptuous and, under black mink,
stark naked.

Let's

Let's drive around
in a bashed-in van, stand
on a collapsing porch at 11 a.m.
draining a can of beer,
lean from an upper window
of the North Star Hotel
counting the days to
welfare. Let's
keep nothing but a wounded
suitcase full of letters, sleep
under the trestle by the river
where old men cast hooks
to scavenger fish. Let's wear
Goodwill clothes that don't
match. Let's
kiss in the shadow
of the foundry, tear up
schedules and maps.
This town is dead.
Let's stay here always.
Arms linked, strutting
our so-whats, let's go
around and around
like a hot watch
killing time.

Spell Against Weather

The wind beats on my windows
with its raw fists.

I will
bake bread, make
magic with yeast and flour
and the dance of my wrists.

See, how in the shiny tins
it doubles in an hour.

Outside, the bleak
trees posture, black on grey,
grainy as newsprint.

I sing over stone-ground wheat.

The oven casts its
aura of heat
like a spell I used to
memorize.

O rise. Rise
fat loaves.
My pots of honey wait.

The odor of this is good.

Beyond the glass
the wood blackens,
starless,
haunted by owl and bat.

Come in. Come in.
Sit
here in my warm kitchen.
Let me
fatten you.

Epidemics

Sleeping with anyone leaves you menaced
by the warfare of desire.
Its contagion flows mouth
to mouth
with the fluency of a language
whose word for love is universal.
Who can trust the body
opening its arms to the enemy?

The sickness crawls over the map,
the aged gasp, their lungs filling
with blue flowers.
Children blaze in their beds
like pots of geraniums.
At night the houses open
in a pitfall of coughing
no sleep is deep enough to rescue.

You see your lovers awakening
with the ravines of their throats
ravaged by fire. You pour water
on the roof of your skull.

In the trenches of no-man's-land,
the plague invades your dreams.
There is no vaccine for this; only
memory can save you.

The Disaster Plan

Remember the swimmer who
came up fast under the ropes
to put his face into a propeller,
blood obscuring the worst.

The gymnast that missed
his timing and landed queerly,
how he was propped forever
sipping liquids.

Or the crash victim
who lay for hours
while the radiator boiled
into his eyes.

None of these people were wicked.
Don't talk to me of consequence.
Your words whine
like an ambulance in my ears.

You say we've arrived at the place
where the bludgeoned girl
was found.

I tell you that lightning
struck our house,
that I didn't arrange
to hurt you.

Red Lake

You are flying to Red Lake,
a place beyond roads,
where the pontoons will let you
glide over the water like Christ.

You said you doubt
I'll miss you. I was still angry
when you disappeared in clouds.
Now that bad mortar crumbles
from my tongue, there are no phones
to drive our voices back and forth like pistons.

I imagine it is green and deep
in the woods, how your hook
hits the water camouflaged in lures,
that at night you drink whiskey
and talk a language given to men
without women.
        I didn't think I'd miss you
until the moon drew a large zero
over my sleep.

Even wounds can keep us running like nurses
to apply the bandages of ourselves.
The most imperative sound is
a siren, the red revolving light
a beacon we can't resist.

Assuredly, the stars command your attention
at Red Lake
as they never do here,
blunted and dulled by the
flash of the city.

I think how your canoe
must slice the dark water like Russian bread,
how the loons will be fishing,
their black necks striking like snakes,
their eerie cries like a hysterical woman
whose man has walked out for good.

I think of the trees like children
who love to play with fire,
white birches, black spruce,
the firs assembled like trolls.

I wonder if you think of me
as the plane drones over
an endless stretch of green
broken only by blue stones glittering
semiprecious, glacially cold.

You are 39 this summer.
I know you are afraid of flying,
afraid of too many roads
converging,
afraid of never going
anyplace.

Unroofed

The Ashanti believe the spirit-people
live in roofless dwellings,
so to dream
of a house without a roof signifies
the death of something.

Perhaps this is why,
when the great beams creak
in the wind at night
and the shingles rattle
like vicious tongues,
I turn to see if you
are sleeping, if your eyes
are moving under their little roofs.

In the corner of our room
there is a leak,
a stain on the plaster, a
weak place where the rain intrudes.
Though you crawl precariously
along the ridge,
searching for a broken slate
or missing flashing,
you can't find the cause...

In every storm we watch it
widen implacably, beyond the art
of fixing. I see the skull behind your face.
You shudder from the ghost
within my heart. At night we dream a twister
is opening our house
like a coffin lid.

Flights

The cardinal wings the early morning
a red question flashing
in and out of leaves.

At noon, the hawk
stabs the sign of the cross
black in the heavens.

Crows at dusk
scatter up like ashes
from the sun's bonfire.

The great horned owl
glides into midnight
on feathers of silence.

We spread our arms
nothing   nothing
so we roost in each other.

Marriage

In the night
my leg slides over your hip
of its own volition,
calf muscles tightening
against the small of your back,
scooping your body
to mine. Half rousing, you
moan, grow hard
against my pelvic bone.
I tremble into wakefulness.

Damn leg of mine,
forgetting
how I fell asleep
on an iceberg of anger
white as this sheet
we're pushing off.

Last Supper

Dinner bell.
Things come hot
from the oven.

Steam rises. The vegetable
curls in a boil of juice
like an infant weary of crying.

The meat oozes
blood. The radish rose
sets its thorn for the tongue.
We talk
divorce. The lettuce faintly rusts
under a cleaved peach
so sweet it cloys.

Once only friends broke bread
or passed the salt.

We've vanquished
custom,
not eating at the same time
from one day to the next.

You'll be here when
I see you. I'll
promise nothing. None
of the silver matches. Most
of the glasses have shattered.

The platter cracks
into hemispheres
beneath its cargo.

Go ahead. Help
yourself. Take up
your knife and fork.

From

CHAGALL POEMS

The Seven Deadly Sins Press, 1980

Song of Songs

The man creeps headfirst out of the bed of roses.
This is how beautiful women
are taken unawares.

They sleep above Byzantine cities
while a severed hand
grasps for the moon.

The woman dreams of
an empty throne. She dreams a king
with wings is playing a golden harp

and all her unborn children
are crawling toward her on their hands and knees.
She likes the way they approach
cowed and obedient.

She likes the red goat
who is eyeing her naked body.

The goat begins to eat
her bed of roses. She thinks he is a god
with a beautiful profile.

He eats the two roses of her nipples.
She shuts her eyes and loves him.

Peasant Life

Feed sugar beets to the white horse,
dance on the blue mountain,
talk beneath the lamp
on a winter evening.

Let the little horse
draw your grandfather up to the moon.
A kind man guides his wagon.

You are not sorry.
Your red cap and pug nose
prepare you to tackle anything.
What do you have to know?

Only this. Let a tree grow in your mind.
Follow the footprints
leading up to the sky. It is your life
ahead of you.

The Magician

Whenever the magician snaps his fingers,
a man and a woman lie down together.
The man is lost in love.
The woman winks.

The magician knows another trick.
In this one there are red flowers
to draw the eye from a sleeping city.

Love supplants government.
It knows the powers
of distraction. You only think
this benevolent bearded man is the magician.

His indigo alter-face
lurks in the wings.

Think of a man's white rabbit.
It disappears
in a woman's black hat.
Everyone gasps.

They want the commonplace
to be extraordinary.
The magician obliges.

The man and woman fall in love.
It lasts.

Poems

A candle
with a man and a woman breathing
over it. Its flame what they think.

The ancestor of time
raises its thin black arms in surrender,
its gold heart throbbing.

Nothing can be stopped.
Christ walks through the world
with his cross grown to his body,

a freak of love and redemption.
Who can guess what he wants?

The child of every man is a ghost
who lives in the moon of his eye.
The book is open. Look!

From
DREAM TREE

Jump River Press, 1980

May

Unlucky month.
The mayflower brings misfortune
into your house.

Begin nothing.
Take no lover.
Birth no child.

The earth is tolling
into flower.
You have no time.

Don't look up. A magpie
might be flying
the sign of your death.

Don't look down.
Mice, souls of the murdered,
are swarming over your shoes.

Find a rusty nail
and carry it with you
throughout the month of May.

The obese goddess
will forget you. She will plod
into orchards and plowed fields

and you can slip
through the numbered leaves
with armfuls of roses.

History of the World

If it is possible to trust the love of an animal,
if it is possible to tell your grief to a stranger,
then you can remember the love of hollyhocks,
those huge blooms primitive as the fear of snakes,
how they stared into your eyes long ago
until the hair rose on your flesh
like the hair of their stalks.

You can remember how the moon laid its white
finger across your lips as you slept,
how a child guards its secrets,
the shoebox of feathers and stones.

You grew between your bones like a ruler
until only sad movies could star your tears.
You wept for the censored scenes, the evidence
that your signature was becoming distinctive.

You discovered that blur could be
defeated with magnification. All haloes
vanished, the ghoul-closets closed.
You obeyed signs, asked directions.

But your lovers betray you. The bread
falls from your fingers to be snatched by white birds
with hard ruby eyes. Underground graffiti
mocks your love of language. The ceilings
are a sluice of rain. You toss sleepless
in strange beds. Loneliness
is finding how you can't befriend yourself.

You dream kittens mew at your threshold, fledglings
pulse, pink and rubbery in the hidden nest,
and strangers open their arms to receive you,
pulling on familiar faces like thugs drawing nylons
over their features. Even this dream escapes your memory.

You rise to a window paling with dawn to see
a doe feeding by the fence
trusting the season with her life.

Two Lizards

One turns green with
rage or fright,
an explicit language.
The other remains brown
as the twig he wants to dominate;
blood pulses the pouch of his throat,
huge as a blown rose.
They move in slow jerks
to the cold-blooded tempo
of time.

The green one retreats
like clockworks,
step by measured step.
The one whose confidence
assumes the coloration
of his stance throbs
like a native drum.

Elongated black
eyespots appear.
Terror masks. A code
of anger, intimidation.

The green one can be seen
anywhere. It has forgotten
how to resemble stones,
sticks. It mottles nervously,
approaching the dish
of mealworms where the other stands
like a sentinel.

Later, the night chill
identifies this lack:
the ability to manufacture warmth.
They blanket each other
along the twig, claws
clutching like all the cold and lonely
whose true colors have been revealed.

Northwood

Sleep anywhere.
The rain will find you
even in the trees.

Later stars,
each a white tooth,
will bite into the black crust.
You'll wake to their hunger.

The breakers on the rock beach
will keep the rhythm
of your dream all night.

Owls will glide over you
in a perfect indifference:
your life
as small a fragment
of everything,
as the monarch butterfly
drowsing on milkweed
or the slag from the old smelter
on the beach path.

In the morning, you will find
many beautiful smooth stones.
You must leave them here
or, in your pack,
they will become so heavily yours
you'll curse them.

This is what you can own
without penance:
your body, your wish,
your sorrow.
You will wake and sleep them
everywhere.
The rest you borrow
and put back.

Cover your ashes with sand,
your traces with time.
The sun goes down again
before you know,
and it is time
to find a flat place
by clear water.

The Dream Book

To dream of abundance signifies
the false security of a belief
in the attraction of opposites.
A wedding foretelling death,
imprisonment meaning good luck,
a corpse: longevity, drowning: good news.

Avoid dreaming of eyes
with their attendant evil,
the dark feathers of loss,
grief of injured fingers,
crows black with disgrace
or breaking dishes,
the poverty of lettuce,
danger of pine trees,
the black veil of separation
or the trouble
of a strange bed.

Instead dream of the ivy
of a fortunate marriage,
the oars of safe enterprise,
full moon of fidelity.

Dream of melons, roses, a sailor
bringing good tidings,
of ribbons, ships and strawberries.

Dream of the consolation of violins,
the umbrellas of prosperity,
illustrious pigs, nests full of birds,
the incomparable happiness of
cabbages and anvils.

From

THE ATROCITY BOOK

Lynx House Press, 1986

Suicide of a Five-Year-Old Girl

The ties are like the rungs of the ladder
Jacob saw rising to heaven.
Between them, white stones
like tears petrified by history.
Imagine the steel rails
reflecting perspective
as they shoot toward the horizon like an arrowhead.

The child lies in bed crying
in the dark. She remembers
reassurance, how everyone is born again
in the spirit. The shape of her hand
is like a bird's tail feathers.
She knows her shoulder blades
could root with wings.

When her eyes, close the stars
descend to the ceiling
of her sight; she flushes through erasure
untugged by admonition.
A light surrounds her
until like angels
she can shed the mangle
of blood and meat
in a rumble of wheels and shriek of air brakes
with a hundred faces pasted
to windows flying awestruck
over her.

The Atrocity Book

Mary Ellen, when your parents went out
we would get the huge illustrated
book from your father's study
and pour over the horrible pictures
of Nazi atrocities.
The best one
was of the young Resistance girl
whose left breast had been slowly burnt off
and still she would not confess.
Her eyes were heroic
but we looked mainly at that
charred, mutilated breast,
our own little buds
full of coals.

We always did this in secret
as if the book were a manual of sexual technique
like the one my mother seized from us,
her mouth a razor slit.

We'd flip through the dead Jews
stacked like rolled newspapers
and find her, our heroine of horror.
Sometimes, we'd take off our clothes
and inspect our perfect bodies.
O, we were glad it was her,
not us, but it had happened
so it could again. We remembered
the holy martyrs, Catherine and her wheel,
Joan and the pyre, how from the prayer-book pictures
they gazed serene, unblemished,
the instruments of the anguish
sanctified.
They bored us now with their
acquiescence, their docile halos.
We wanted the real thing.
The scream frozen. The eyes
famished of hope.

The body twisted
like suffering Jesus
in the painting by Grunewald.

How it felt, how it felt
we wondered, twitching
with excitement.

O Musselmen,
we had not the slightest compassion
for your skeletal numbness
but leaned, two cleavers
of honed curiosity,
to chop your torment in half
and analyze it, touch it.

And that blackened chewed-up breast,
we loved it.

All these years later
I think about
why your father had that book,
why we risked censure
to look at it avidly, often
why I am
writing this poem.

Freakshow

I: The Crocodile Lady

This is my skin.
Reptilian.
I am sister
to lizard, alligator,
the dragons of Komodo.

I sit here above you
in bra and panties,
watching you look and shudder.

Do you long to touch me?

Your squeamish urge
leaves me cold
as the great glacier.

I am the last
dinosaur,
so large with sorrow
the world
cannot hold me.

II: Fat Lady

I am the complete
book of curves.
I have no
right angles, am
a sole lushness
of flesh, fold on fold.

Dress me
in ruffles and rouge.
I am that fat baby
you long to be once more.
I kiss and scold.

My voice
all gurgles,

that language
you thought you'd forgotten.

Call me gross.

But I am so sweet and milky
with my splurge
you can't help but
love me.

III: *India Rubber Boy*

Your mind can't
stretch the way I pull
my cheek and let
its elastic snap.

Seize me anywhere
and I ease
from your hand.

You rigid others
living in skins
like sausages.

I am so unconfined
I can shuck your briefcases,
topcoats and time-clocks,
get paid for nothing
but to sit here
letting you rubbereye.

IV: *The Giant*

According to the old stories,
my race was first.
Our names a gargle
of consonants.
Mountains were made for us.
We lived happy as boulders.

But the little people
who can never let anything alone

came armed with craft
and duplicity against our enormous
innocence.
Now the world I live in
is theirs.
I bump my head
on their ceilings,
burst from their clothes,
my feet
hang out of their beds.

My magnitude astounds them first,
then they walk
at their own eye-level
making bad jokes
that bounce off my belt buckle.

I could crush them
but I don't.

I am the last magnanimous man
and I won't
live long.

V. *The Sword Swallower*

It's just technique,
practice, a skill
that can be learned.

The steel
no longer gags me
but slips
through my gullet like a worm.

I tilt my head back—
how you crowd to see
if I'll be split
from sternum to crotch.

Not me.
I'm good at this.

It's a skill I learned.
I could be elsewhere.

It's just a matter of technique.

They pay me for it.
I keep the muscles lax
and do what I am good at.

I'm no freak.

Palmistry

Groping through ground fog
risen to white
obliteration,
only the hand comes clear.

Geographic.
A map of an unknown country.
Hills and hollows
unexplored and forbidding
limned with red tracks,
we follow blindly
groping and stumbling.

This is the mind line.
It runs unswerving
to an outer limit
and falls off,
come to nothing.

Next the heart line
forking with indecisions.
It is broken and broken.
Still it picks up
and goes on.

The fate line
vagues to a series
of whimsies, each brief
and inconclusive.

And now the lifeline
long and checkered
with disaster and salvation.

It rounds
the opposing thumb
(exquisite technical asset
of industrial intelligence)

and peters out,
lost in obscurities
and bad debts.

With this palm
we disarm enemies,
hold out
for gain or friendship.
Caress or slap,
smooth both.

It tells us
where we were, are,
and what next,
if we could only decipher
its cryptic
treasure map.

Find the tall pine
and rotting corpse
that guards the buried casque
brimming with
emeralds and bones.

The fog thickens.
The landscape closes.
All that can be seen
is the hand
before the face.

"a banner
with the strange device"

The Disgrace

...we've never been women, we've never been nobodies
—from "Ancestors" by Cesar Pavese

Tough, sinewy, at eleven
I was terrified of breasts,
those loose
globes of flesh
bouncing on the thin
washboard of my chest
as I set my chestnut mare
at the triple bar.

Horror
growing upon my body
like soft fists fit
for the fists and mouths of men.

Saying no, I
strutted, swaggered my lean hips
in blued-out jeans,
skinny brown arms
steering the flight of geldings,
the dance of my round-rumped mare
flirting her flax tail
at the chained stud
who whickered and burned.

I spurred her to the
tangled wood where wildflowers
were snapping out from every crevice.
My narrow buttocks
settled into the rhythm of a
hand-gallop. Later
first blood crusted my thighs.
There was no hope.

I was about
to be turned into a woman,
a nobody,
a body I would live behind

that men would want for its own sake,
for its bubble breasts
and jiggly thighs.

I ran my hands
over my flat-muscled flanks
toughening against
the desire to cry out
like a weak creature,
a woman, a nobody.

Evening—1943

Jailed in lampglow, Father
is brooding over Gibbon
in his yellow leather chair
as, jarred with static
on our shortwave radio,
some guttural country utters
the consonants of war.

Belly down on our brown rug,
I watch the console's grid
allow the pointer-tongue to glide
through weather, news and drama.

Father's pages turn in clock-time
as the bridge-lamp leans to see
his bare silver-dollar spot,
his rimless glasses mirroring
the mantel and blue serpents of
gas fire in their white-brick nest.

His nose goes down in
three small humps,
each of which has
its own shine.

I let the Zenith suck me in
through its vents of webbed design.
The Voice of Firestone strikes the night
to a flare of violins
as Father in his hearth-fire plot
goes knee-crossed into the Decline.

Pioneering the Heartland

For years
we slept on the staked plain
where only the scavenging wind endures.
It still
shrieks in my ears like the banshees
in the abandoned shacks where we stayed
until the floorboards disappeared
like dust devils.

Then we'd load our gear
onto the buckboard and head
for someplace we'd already been.

Recognize the cabin
where porcupines were scouring the shelves for salt.
Find the burial place
overgrown with weeds
where we held hands and wept
until our eyes dried up,
until the sun
turned the land to chalk
and the water wasn't
fit to drink.

It was some time after that
you flogged the roan mare to death
and I broke my looking glass.

In bed
your whiskey breath
sours on my mouth.
My body is the hollow
you root for like a bear
when winter comes.

At sunrise there are buzzards
circling in the air
and we've eaten all our seed corn.

Grandfather

Story running through my childhood:
trapped by a cattle guard,
gun in hand aimed
at the man who will kill you,
you are transformed
from ordinary forebear
whose name and face lingers
in unopened albums
into a legend of summer evenings
told by father to daughter
in a flat land
bearing no resemblance
to your cottonwood mountains.

This single violent act
has made you memorable.
Nothing else
is verified—though it is said
you were always a wanderer;
children buried
in the places you left:
Texas, Oklahoma, New
Mexico territory.

Your wife would only tell
her children that
you were innocent when you died.
And they hung the man who shot you
so we may infer
your respectability, a victim of
terrible circumstances; but why
running like that, gun in hand,
grandfather, when they got you?

It doesn't matter.
We don't judge you
or know you or
really care.

But we remember you
and tell you
on childhood's porches
until you have become
our Western Epic.

Midnight Rhumba

I sway in the dark
with a basket of fruit on my head
like Carmen Miranda
doing the rhumba on the late movie
before I was even
born.

The dead appear on the screen
as they do in dreams,
their faces insisting on
immortality. I've tried forgetting
but every night you're back.

Sometimes you slip your skin
like a snake and turn into
some other lover who also
hurt me—it's not who you were,
it's what you made me feel.

Be nameless then.
I won't disclose your secrets.
The palette knife sticky with gore,
the anonymous letter,
the marionette who looked like me.

Your voice still ringing
in my ears like nickels and dimes
in a pay phone.

Your eyes off-green as
counterfeit money.

Lie down in your deathbed.
The accident happened.
I got over this long ago
so why have you come
cheek-to-cheek
like Cesar Romero
to dance me through this sleep,
my head crowned with

oranges, bananas,
your hair penguin-sleek.
We were never like this
no matter how we
pretended.

Mulberries

Purple chandeliers.
Gather them, gather them.
Your hands stained,
an investment of blood,
black tears
shed over nothing.

I can tell who you are,
your lips inked
with more than words or kisses.
Each gatherer
recognizes a friend climbing into the trees
to contend with birds.

This is the crooked tree
beloved of silkworms.
This is the ancient tree
grubbed out by gardeners
and classed as a marauder
like ailanthus, the tree of heaven.

You were taught never to eat
such berries. You were told
how cultivation secures history,
how you could be discovered,
gory-mouthed and ravenous,
your fists oozing with menstrual blood.
The trees shook castanets
of pigeon-blood rubies
black-red as original sin,
as lust, as revolution.

You fill your shirt like the children,
indifferent to stain. I tell you we'll
make wine, conserves of this. Look,
wild in the fields, how the trees rampage,
dark jewels braided in their manes.
Yours, mine
for the gathering.

From
THE LONELY HEARTS KILLERS

Spoon River Poetry Press, 1986

For a Girl Found Strangled in a Cornfield

Girls on bicycles
pedal aimlessly along blacktop roads
between rows of head-high corn
whose green plumage
stutters the wind.
The afternoon falls to shadow.

Leaving her homing friends,
the last girl rides
into the melting heart of blackness
where tree and road
erase each other.

Her bicycle is found here.

The prudent girls
in morning living rooms
dumbly shake their heads,
imagining her
groping through the file
of green-black spears
ranging to a ripeness
she feels possess her,
a legacy of earth
she cannot decipher but yearns for.

Someone watches, smiles, moves in upon her.

A root of fear
and anticipation holds her
transfixed
to a starry night
gone still
while all the lush-leaved stalks
part to reveal her
paralyzed with moonlight
like a prayer
no one has ever heard.

This is where they find her.

The Lonely Hearts Killers

—Raymond Fernandez and Martha Beck

Irresistible charm. He can
mesmerize with words.
They plunge from the page
into the blue veins of widows,
ooze into pale blue ink.
These women's hands
describe ovals in the air,
fly to him like homing birds.

One of the first,
an obese nurse named Martha,
recognizes his genius.

They make a pair:
His come-ons,
her greed.
O Love and Money.

He marries the lonely widows.
She slams them with a hammer
into a final solitude. They bury
victims in cellars of rented houses,
count the fleeced life savings,
go to the cinema
where Cary Grant cocks a suave eye
and Barbara Stanwyck murmurs throatily.

A psychiatrist might tell us
Raymond's problems date
from a shipboard accident
and Martha's from being raped
at 13 by her brother.

About the victims?
Somebody died on them. They were
lonely. Explanations, like reasons,
come after the fact. The act

of kissing the plump lady,
bashing her head in.

Eating popcorn while the black-and-white
figures prance and prattle. Which life is real?
She's crazy about him.
He loves her back, all 280
voluptuous pounds.

The police are waiting
when they return from the movies
laughing, gobbling chocolate kisses.

She gives the scandal sheets a treat:
her overactive glands drove her
into his arms. Twenty other women
fell just as hard, but forever.

Some of their bones exhumed, others
vanished. There's proof enough.
They get the chair.

She knows he loves her.
He knows she's been true.
Jerk and blaze
in one last intimacy
all they've been through.

Now each lonely
heart shudders and fails.
Witnesses button their overcoats,
walk to their cars.
             Rain falling on Sing Sing.
O Lonely Hearts.

The Monster of the Andes

—Pedro Alonzo Lopez

I cannot see a star above me.
My mother left me
in a town 80 miles from my birthplace.
I never saw her again. I am
a seventh son abandoned by God
and the Madonna.

Guards stare through these bars.
One night
they will slip into my cell with knives
to mutilate my body.
              No sunlight.
No air.
              I cannot sleep in this closed room.

Once I walked through the markets
seeking a girl
with a certain look on her face
of innocence and beauty.
When her mother left her alone
for a moment, I would give her a mirror,
take her by the hand to a place
of concealment. All night she would sleep
trustingly as a daughter in my arms.

I waited until daylight
to kill them.
              Those delicate girls,
their round brown arms
and slender throats. My hands
fit them like silver necklaces.
I kissed their eyes
into oblivion.

When they were missed
it was thought
they had been coerced as maids to the rich.
              They were better off

servants to my obsession,
laughing as I described the presents
we would buy in Lima,
in Quito, in Bogota.
            They lie beneath paved roads
in secrecy
as they had to lie beneath my body
crying out for stars
as I cried
when the Indians were burying me alive.

Now this darkness
where I cannot rest.
A place of women too old
to want. I glower
through the iron slit,
three graven lines raying
above my eyes like the sun
I can no longer imagine.

This is wrong, this captivity, this isolation,
the trial I await thinking
how the pregnant river
swirled into those graves to betray me.

O furious mother,
it is the breastless I want,
pure girls without body hair,
girls who offer up their eyes to heaven
knitting with the earth beneath my plunge
into death, into love.

A man like you and you
like anyone
            who exists to feel something.

Dr. Beaumont

His misfortune
made my career.

Stomach shot,
I declared him dead
in 36 hours.

But he lived down my words.

It was I
who saved him,
feeding him through his asshole
until the wound
almost closed.

But not entirely.
Not entirely.

That was the marvel,
a little window
into his belly

through which I could peer,
observing the entire
gastric process.

I used to suspend
bits of bread and meat
to watch the juices flow.
I paid him more for this
than he could trap

and wrote
the bible on digestion.

To be fair,
I'll grant him credit
for being there
when the shotgun accidentally
discharged.

But his contribution
was always reluctant.

Though I saved him to sire
seventeen brats
and gave him cash money
to let me look in there,
in that small fascinating
mouth,
he ran off.

The rest of my life I spent
searching for him.

A Man of Science.

Wedding Pictures—Grandparents, 1891

The setting is classic: your bride
radiates contentment. Her silks fold about her,
softly formal. Each button strains
smugly over her breast.
Her hands close on life,
smooth and boneless.

How clear her gaze is,
brown as an animal's
and as sure.
Domesticity becomes her.
She looks ready to step firmly
into your life together,
flouring her hands.

You, however, in cravat
and graveyard suit,
rangy, crow-wing hair blown back,
look as wild-eyed and hag-ridden
as our black Labrador when he came
back from a week-long dosing of arsenic
at the vet.

As I look at you, nervous, ready
to leap out of this photograph
into some other frame of mind,
I see it was the heartworm
had you both. Poor dog, poor man.

I'm not surprised you died young,
shot five times,
or that in Utah,
waiting with her children,
your resolute wife
heard the news, swept the dirt floor,
and began anew to
plan her life.

The Study of Astronomy

My father, in old age, is obsessed
with stars,
cosmic mysteries, how light
travels through space from exploded suns,
how constellations
form and solar systems,
galaxy after galaxy, recurrence of comets,
timeliness of meteors,
possibilities of black holes.

My father reveres the novae
of Tycho Brahe
visible in full daylight,
the envelope of Nova Persei,
the supernovae of 1006
in the constellation Lupus,
the wolf star.

He writes about the runaway stars
flying from their orbits
to race through black fields of space
like white horses,
of the process of infall,
the red shift of quasars.

He says he needs to know
the laws that govern stars—theories
of creation, dissolution—because he is getting old
and there is not much time now
to wish on the first star
or the falling star.

Rose Red to Snow White

A dark wind batters the door.
Our minds unchink as
the chimney roars and the eaves
shriek in their rusty dreams.

Huddle by the fire, sister.
Something is snapping in the applewood
and sparks ignite our nightgowns.
Let us save each other.
Let us marry these ashes.

Don't leave the comfort we've found
for that rap on the doorjamb.
God knows who'd be out
on such a night, in a blizzard
like this one. Have no pity
on travelers far from town
in this fierce weather.

But you've unlatched us,
let a whirlwind of white flakes
confuse our destinies
and succored a brute of fur
whose snout embeds
in your fabulous hair.

A thorn stabs
my red heart
as you lie down
with the great bear,
bringing him to life
with your white body.

How can you be sure
he'll turn at last into something
noble, that he won't always
raid your breasts for honey
or sleep grunting all winter?

The Icon of Our Lady of Perpetual Help

A Byzantine lack of perspective
confuses the child in her arms.
A shrunken adult
infused with the sanctity
of an unearthly man. Redeemer.

Real infants are large-skulled,
their eyes shallow ponds
glinting with light. This holy one
is too alert, fox-smart, wears
a golden circlet of brilliance
like a baptismal cap.

The mother inclines to the right,
the ancient posture of sorrow.
Black veil, wimple
white and boneless as her hands
clasping the child in resignation.
Folds of her gown
falling in classic
restrictions. A crown of intricate stars
lacy and illusive as fishbones.

Two seraphim uphold her halo,
a single gold line.
With bird-of-prey wings,
bodies limbless as mermaids,
they pause beautifully
in mid-air like dragonflies.

Gilt frame, jewel tones,
little man stiff as a puppet,
mother of acquiescence,
simplest response to hope
stuck on hut walls or enshrined
in nine-domed cathedrals, O Lady
of Perpetual Help.

Bees

For Sylvia Plath

The honeycomb we brought up from the hive
last night and set on the back stoop
is stripped of honey this morning. A few bees
still trundle heavy-winged through the wood,
restoring lost treasure. Bees
function as one idea, so we are told,
each a facet of the whole as fingers,
elbows, eyes, are appurtenances of the body.

We must remember to speak politely
in the presence of bees. If anyone dies,
we must remember to tell them
or they might defect. Fly off,
bearing away all sweetness.

We know
they don't blossom from the carcasses
of lions or oxen as our forefathers guessed.
This is how they arrive. Boxed up. Then released
into the world, a thousand plagues,
and we are Pandoras, gullible, curious,
shaking an empty carton thinking hope,
as in the legend, will be a kind of insect
instead of a thing our tongues must learn to shape
and utter in the worst of times.

In the worst of times, in the dynasty of
Chaos, the infant Zeus
was guarded by sacred bees.
He grew into the primacy of light.
Father. Bee-Man.

Source of mead. Honeyed tongue
of gods and poets.
Write a text on bees. Mother them
swathed in white veils,
a terrible buzz of infancy,
of the world at creation.

What next?
Who told the hive?
Anyone? Anyone?

What bee danced the story
of our theft last night?
The hive resonant with loss
and a furious resolve. A few bees
circle the steps. Herculean task.
O Queen of the isolate chamber
dreaming the rest to worship,
to obligation, to oblivion.
We depart from here
empty-handed.

In the picture on our wall
Lord Krishna
in the guise of a bee
rests on a lotus blossom.
Feeling foolish, I tell him
Sylvia Plath is dead.

True Love

You enter this country like a priest,
knowing it won't be easy.
The old tales of torment echoing in your ears,
how the natives
will make you suffer in proof of devotion,
the terrible creed of an alien culture
that honors the silent bearing of pain.

The others, expedient explorers
out for gold, fueled with rumors
of lost cities,
will tell your story over campfires,
understanding nothing of your obsession.

You walk loudly through the forest
to notify the villages,
animals streaking from your footfall.
Almost immediately you are lost.

Hunger will be gripping your stomach
by the time dark hands lead you
into the clearing. You don't know
the word for water. They don't know
the word for compassion.

How can you teach them by example
when they respect only stoicism?
It is love, passionate as the love
of holy Christ, you yearn
to fold over their nakedness.

These savages
driving slivers under your fingernails,
slitting your nostrils,
until at last you wish to give nothing,
only to save yourself. It is then
one slides her round arms about your neck.

From
DEAD HORSES

FutureCycle Press, 2012

Drought

The wells went dry, then the rivers
Lessened to a trickle and disappeared,
Leaving only indentations studded with pebbles
And the occasional boulder.

We sent the cattle to slaughter rather than watch them die of thirst.
Chickens scratched a pointless calligraphy in bare earth and ants
Caravanned through clapboards, not for sugar
But for water.

Now the water witch dances with his willow rod,
Comes up with nothing, his arms numb with loss.
Levels of everything diminish. Even tears
Clog in our ducts, leaving us red-eyed and sorry.

Our pockets, once jingling with hope,
Are full of sand. Scorpions
Crawl where the wisteria used to flower
Over the old pergola. Every afternoon
Clouds float over, empty as pillowcases.

Chac, god of rain, frowns on the Mayan virgins,
Throws his sacks of water over his shoulder and stomps off.
Their bones in the empty wells mean nothing,
Mean less than nothing.
Lining up the constellations
Fails to help.

The dust storms drive everyone to the sea
Where the pickings are slim, the water
Murderous. On the weather maps,
A fiery splotch promises more of the same.

What can we give each other
Besides the names of every kind of water
Into which we ever dipped our hands—
The Great Lakes, the springs, the creeks, the rivers—
And always the blessing of the rain.

Pay attention now. Look for one
Green thing to remember.

Dead Horses

Now that they are dead or gone, the dream
Is always of a field where running horses
Flash past, hooves catching and echoing light,
The grass lush, milkweed or Queen Anne's lace
Along the fencerows. Then suddenly it's winter,
Snow is falling, shapes are haloed, the sky is bleak.

You might awaken, amazed the sound of horses
Has passed, diminished just as a streak of daylight
Pours through the curtains, fills bastions of lace
As your eyes fill with sorrow recalling a winter
Where nothing ever thawed, each vista bleak.
You knew the vault of loss, the end of dreams,

But would not acknowledge it, that blight of light
Unraveling the seams of some grandmother's lace
Concoction that formed a history, that overwintered
In every house you slept in, every bleak
Ceiling that you woke to, emptying dreams
Into a landscape now bereft of horses.

Those horses: the dappled one like old lace
Fading into the slushy nouns of winter,
Its whites and blacks and greys as bleak
As a deserted park, no childhood dreams
Anchored by swingsets or gymnastic horses
On which you vaulted, slim and young and light

As any snowflake in any kind of winter,
The brilliant sled-filled one, even the bleak
Fog-frosted dawns, the ones that hid all dreams
Until they burst from the icy mists like horses
Racing to the barns in that first light
Presaging hunger, muzzles coated with the lace

Of their breathing, how they stormed the bleak
Hollows where your final splintered dreams
Corroded. You want them now, those horses
Crashing the earth with sound as if light

Had been surpassed by speed, as if the laces
That bind you to your bones gave way to winter's

Blast, unreining every dream, freeing the horses
Of your past, lightening that blanket of heavy lace
Until you open your arms to winter and everything holy or bleak.

The Lunar Year

Hunger Moon

That's when the food ran out. The stock
Depleted, even the saved potatoes gone,
Rotten at the eyes. Our savings cleft
By half, all love foreclosed, the doors
Of home padlocked, the windows boarded.
What else can happen? Weather broods
Over the bleak horizon. This moon is also known
As the snow moon.

Crow Moon

The raven invented the world. Now the crow rules
Its lesser partitions. It encompasses
The slyness of politicians, the ruthlessness of love.
It waits for things to die or else it torments
Songbirds, those who can tongue
A harmony every crow despises.

Egg Moon

The lost wax process creates an egg
Of gorgeous dimensions, Byzantine
Geometrics suggesting a rage of contained
Passion. But another egg is pure.
Cool in the palm and distant
As that place where everything begins.

Milk Moon

It is this specialization that defines us.
How we link to every creature
That nurses its young. That
Baptismal drink the Orient refuses
After a certain age. What sort of wisdom
Clinks bottles on a stoop at dawn
Like earliest, beloved memories.

Strawberry Moon

You find them knitting the pasture
With rubies, the wild sort
Whose sweetness is so compact, so perfect
That cultivation seems a sort of sin,
Original as the path that led us out
Of infancy to the bloody-hearted world,
Wearing its seeds like a cloak.

Thunder Moon

Everything here depends on nitrogen
Of which thunder is merely the voice,
As a slap is the sound of forked anger,
The sound angels made as they fell
Into the firmament. The first denial.

Sturgeon Moon

Producers of caviar and isinglass,
One richly edible, the other a bonding agent
Like the lust that glues two lovers.
Flesh of temperate waters. The miracle
That feeds a jubilation
Of disbelievers. Cast your net. Have patience.

Barley Moon

All grains were once wild,
Uncultivated, there for the reaping,
There for the first lively spirits
Fermenting like every wish into
Something achievable, the malt
Of high ambition.

Harvest Moon

Every goddess walks
Under that parasol, her arms
A cornucopia of fulfillment.
No wonder we worship this

Unblemished guise. No wonder
We think no matter how many banks
Fail, how many ships break into pieces
In the coming gales, we'll still
Have this: how we were blessed
Just as the good times ended.

Hunter's Moon

That's what we do when everything
We counted on has collapsed
And all coffers are empty, all drawers
Divested of silk, all trigger fingers
Reinvested with darkness. Walk
Silently in the tracks of the dispossessed,
Ensuring it will not be you.

Cold Moon

Hunker down. Survival is now the key
To your heart, the tone-deaf song.
If you make a fire it is certain
To go out while you're asleep.
You'll wake with your feet frozen
In a crossroad of bad choices.
Shaking is the way your body
Fights cold like this. Huddle together.

Wolf Moon

They have come back, those predators
Of the prairie, the steppe, the open range,
Protected as a parliament
Of oligarchs, their guard hairs rising
As they sight you, out there
In your unarmed villages.

Roadkill

Dead skunk on the road.
One hundred degrees, the stink is bad.
The county should be out
To scrape it up, but after two days
We take our shovels to it.

Traveling north, another skunk
Creased in the highway. Twin kittens
Pawing helplessly at her.
The kids beg us to stop.
We explain why not and drive on.

Everywhere are deer, muskrats,
Raccoons, possums, cats, even birds
Flying too low or alighting
On something already killed,

Blacktop littered as if
Figments of imagination
Had spun off to sizzle
Under a July sun.

Anesthetized, we hardly comprehend
What these clumps of fur and sinew were,
And we don't much care.

Not like the man, a week ago,
Who, seeing ducklings on the tollway,
Left his car running and rushed
To their rescue. He was hit
Almost at once, then hit again.

Roadkill. Today, a smear
Greyish, flattened. We keep going.

Hammering

My neighbor has been roofing his barn
For the last several weeks,
Down to the bare beams,
Replacing the ruined wood.
His hammer ratchets the morning
Out of the sycamores. It's taking
Him too long, I think, a job
For more than one man. But he's
Industrious. I can see the sheets
Of plywood bright as toffee.
He's got the squares of shingles stacked.
Every night he stretches a blue tarp
Over his handiwork in case of rain.
Every daylight hour, I hear the knock
Of his nails arcing the planes,
And if I walk along the roadside thick
With chicory and wild carrot, I see him
Kneeling at noontide, his muscled forearm
Upraised, about to strike.

Renovations

When we open the wall,
An intricacy of wasps' nests
Like the ruins of Angkor Wat.

Long abandoned, the paper apartments
Collapse at a touch. It's surprising
What is found. The newspapers

Dated 1874 used for insulation
Crumbled to golden dust before
We could read a word.

It's like discovering a journal
You kept years ago. How naïve
You were, but in a way

Heart-breaking as only the young are
In their solemnities.
Or finding a letter you never answered,

And an inked calligraphy
Opens your spirit like an
Exotic bird call.

This is not restoration, this task,
Not duplication of
Historical details.

Instead, a new décor,
A room opening to
Another room for space and light

To see beyond
The papyrus cells
Of memory.

Barn Fire

Green, dense, moist, packed and stacked
Ten high to fill the loft. A narrow aisle
Filters light lauded with dust.
A yeasty smell, good enough to eat
Or kindle. How the heat begins to smolder
Deep, deep within the wick of bale,
A thin snake of smoke like the contrail
Of a high-flying jet echoing
Its sound breaks. Swallow nests,
Then the great beams catch and glow. That's
How it starts, not a cigarette
Discarded or a wire gnawed by rats.
The provender ignites its own safekeeping.
Its axioms of immolation bless
The harvest with a baleful flame. Here's the rest
Of that story—that story
Of storage, of keeping safe, of keeping
Everything inviolate. Each story is a myth
In which someone discovers fire,
And then it all begins.

The Threshing Bee And Steam Show

Clam shell seats have bent them,
Sloped the shoulders shaping a posture:
Old farmer. Short sleeves, striped or plaid,
Pressed dungarees or dark work pants.
Scrawny, arms ropey with lean muscle,
Burnt with a thousand suns.
White-haired or grey, clean-shaven.
John Deere or Seed caps, Red Wing work shoes.

Average age of seventy-plus. Still farming,
Beans or corn. Winter wheat,
Milk cows or custom hay. How many seasons
In the fields astride the tractors
Pulling disc, plow, picker, mower, spreader.
Gripping the wheel, shifting gears,
Down the long rows sunup to sundown,
Cornering at the verge.

In winter barns, they restore
The ancient tractors—the 1940 Allis Chalmers,
The '31 Fordson, the '50 Harvester—
To a pristine condition.

Today, the old tractors shine.
In glossy paint, scrubbed tires, they parade,
The old farmers slumped at the wheels
Steering into applause, waving,
Some faintly smiling, others proudly stern
As if they were still young and tough and upright.

Ox Team at Garfield Farm

Paired shortly after birth.
By two months bearing
The smallest yoke,
Learning the commands
Which nigh ox and off ox
Understand differently,
Always the same position,
Yoked or stalled.
Nigh ox to the right.
Off ox to the left.

Long horns intact
To keep the wooden yoke
In place. Controlled
By voice or motion.
Obedient and calm, their huge
Bodies compliant to plow,
Wagon, or log chain.

The ox driver points out
What fables those Westerns were:
Wagon trains circling
Their handsome horse hitches.

It was oxen
That opened the west,
Able to live on almost nothing,
To unmoor the mired cart,
Plod all day in patience.

No special breed, just
Cattle that were taught
To work. These two are ruddy
And boxlike with fleshy ivory nostrils
And the placid eyes of servants.
Each has one horntip screwed with brass.
Each has a name: Nigh Ox—Off Ox.

They think as an ensemble,
Mirror images of toil.
If one dies, the other is useless.

Two Deaths

I

The hurt owl
In the gravel roadway shifts
From one claw to the other,
The iris of one eye splattered
Like ink on yellow
Cellophane. The other eye
Stares, a perfect target,
Distrustful, woozy.
It has fluffed itself
Big as a tombstone: tufted
Earfeathers, scythe-beak clacking,
Its little tongue snake-pale.

II

The colt is still alive
On his feet, plodding, head down,
In slow circles, fur matted with sawdust,
Eye a prayer of flies.
Chainsawing dullness, legs buckle
Him down into a heap—
Swollen belly, head flung
At a distorted angle.
Last night, he thrashed in the stall
While you inoculated sleep.
A grey-white rat slid past
On a beam above your head, ghostlike.
I held the water bucket
To the colt's lips. You supported
Him as he drank shallowly,
Then sighed and rested
His head on a flake of straw.
Dawn gripped the edges of the window.
Mourning doves began to call.
The colt's sides heaved
And heaved and heaved. He went on breathing.

III

It will be another scorcher. Already, heat
Pleats the inner wrists of willow leaves
And, in the dips of pasture, mist
Is burning off.
You choke a rat
From the white cat's jaws,
A gift of sustenance for the owl
Who perches on a fallen branch in shade,
Lifting one tilted hinge
Lopsidedly as if recalling
Long noiseless swoops from barn to barn
When he was still a menacing shadow.
He accepts the rat
With dignity, his intact eye
An awful inquiry
Fixing ours. The third lid shutters, opaque,
Back and forth over the blasted one,
A yellow map of jagged black islands.
He puffs up big at our approach
But doesn't flee. He is the predator.

IV

The colt sprawls in the sun
In a dome of flies.
Sudden violent twistings, then
Collapse. His huge dark eye,
Moist as a grape, rolls
In terror. His cries
Are silent ones. Just weaned, he's learned
The hopelessness of bawling.
You give him morphine. He doesn't
Want to die, this feisty little one,
Staggering to his tiny hoofs to thrust
His muzzle into water, come up dripping,
Not swallowing, his eyes
Terribly hurt, then down, rolling again,
Learning how to stop living
In the agony of a twisted gut.

V

The backhoe comes to dig him under.
In the far field, mares in foal
Are grazing, and the August sky,
Shorn of clouds, bloats bright blue,
Brash as the barn man with his red muscles
And unblinking pleasant bovine stare.

VI

The owl waits for the long day
To cripple into nightfall.
He won't make it
Either, eyeshot, equilibrium
Vanquished. He ruffles himself
To the largest version of threat he can
And postures furiously against tomorrow.

Acknowledgments

Grateful acknowledgment is made to the following publications in which poems from this collection first appeared, some in slightly different versions: *Albatross, Alembic, Another Chicago Magazine, Ascent, Attention Please, Ballard Street Review, Banyon Anthology, Blackberry, Blue Unicorn, Broadkill Review, Buckle, Butt: A Quarterly, Cape Rock, Chowder Review, Cornfield Review, Disenchantments: An Anthology of Modern Fairy Tale Poetry, Earth's Daughters, East River Review, Fine China: 20 Years of Earth's Daughters Anthology, Gargoyle, Georgia State University Review, Grand Street, Hollins Critic, Images, Iodine Review, Just Pulp, Kudzu, Mississippi Valley Review, the new renaissance. New York Quarterly, Nimrod, North American Review, Panhandler, Passages/North, Phoebe, Poetry on the Bus, Portland Review, Rhode Island Review, Rockbottom, Rocky Mountain Review, Slick Press, Snowy Egret, Sou'wester, Spirit That Moves Us, Spoon River Quarterly, Tinderbox, Urthkin, Washout Review, West Branch, West Conscious Review, West End, Western Humanities Review, What Have You Lost Anthology, Wilderness House, Wisconsin Review, Yes: A Review of Poetry.*

Cover art, "Crow in silhouette," by Andrew Langham; author photo by Nancy Knott; cover and interior book design by Diane Kistner (dkistner@futurecycle.org); Gentium Book Basic text with Cronos Pro titling

About FutureCycle Press

FutureCycle Press is dedicated to publishing lasting English-language poetry and flash fiction books, chapbooks, and anthologies in both print-on-demand and ebook formats. Founded in 2007 by long-time independent editor/publishers and partners Diane Kistner and Robert S. King, the press incorporated as a nonprofit in 2012. A number of our editors are distinguished poets and authors in their own right, and we have been actively involved in the small press movement going back to the early seventies.

The FutureCycle Poetry Book Prize and honorarium is awarded annually for the best full-length volume of poetry we publish in a calendar year. Introduced in 2013, our Good Works projects are devoted to issues of global significance, with all proceeds donated to a related worthy cause. We are dedicated to giving all authors we publish the care their work deserves, making our catalog of titles the most distinguished it can be, and paying forward any earnings to fund more great books.

We've learned a few things about independent publishing over the years. We've also evolved a unique, resilient publishing model that allows us to focus mainly on vetting and preserving for posterity the most books of exceptional quality without becoming overwhelmed with bookkeeping and mailing, fundraising activities, or taxing editorial and production "bubbles." To find out more about what we are doing, come see us at www.futurecycle.org.

The FutureCycle Poetry Book Prize

All full-length volumes of poetry published by FutureCycle Press in a given calendar year are considered for the annual FutureCycle Poetry Book Prize. This allows us to consider each submission on its own merits, outside of the context of a contest. Too, the judges see the finished book, which will have benefitted from the beautiful book design and strong editorial gloss we are famous for.

The book ranked the best in judging is announced as the prize-winner in the subsequent year. There is no fixed monetary award; instead, the winning poet receives an honorarium of 20% of the total net royalties from all poetry books and chapbooks the press sold online in the year the winning book was published. The winner is also accorded the honor of judging the next year's competition.